# The Ultimate *Harry Styles* Book Fan Book

### Harry Styles
### Facts, Photos, Quizzes
### & More

**Jamie Anderson**

**BELLANOVA**

MELBOURNE · SOFIA · BERLIN

Copyright © 2022 by Jamie Anderson

**The Ultimate Harry Styles Fan Book 2022**
www.bellanovabooks.com

All rights reserved. No part of this book may be reproduced in any form by any electronic or mechanical means including photocopying, recording, or information storage and retrieval without permission in writing from the author.

Harry Styles was not involved in the writing of this book. However, all facts are believed to be truthful based on reputable, public domain sources.

**PAPERBACK**
ISBN: 978-619-7695-22-9
Imprint: Bellanova Books

THE ULTIMATE HARRY STYLES FAN BOOK

# Contents

**Introduction** ................................ 6
**Harry: Fun Facts** ........................... 8
**Harry: The Quiz** ........................... 22
    Family & Early Life ..................... 22
    Music & Career ........................... 32
    Private Life .................................. 46
**Harry: The Lyrics Quiz** ...................... 56
**Quiz: Bonus Round** ........................... 64
**Harry: Quotes** ...................................... 71
**Wordsearch** .......................................... 80
**Crossword Puzzle** ............................... 82
**Solutions** .............................................. 84

## *Harry Styles*
# INTRODUCTION

Since auditioning for X-Factor in 2010, Harry Styles has taken over the pop world. First as a member of One Direction, and then as a just-as-awesome solo star.

So how much do you *really* know about Harry? In this book you will learn about Harry's career, what his childhood was like and much more. Are you ready? *Let's go!*

## Harry Styles
# FUN FACTS

Harry's hair wasn't always curly! It was straight until the end of primary school.

• • •

Harry has four nipples! As well as his normal two, he has two extra tiny ones.

• • •

Harry came up with the name One Direction for the band during The X-Factor.

Before The X-Factor, Harry applied for a job as a lifeguard.

• • •

Harry apparently calls his mom up to five times a day. He's a big mommy's boy!

• • •

Harry often talks in his sleep.

• • •

Harry is really good friends with fellow British pop star, Ed Sheeran.

THE ULTIMATE HARRY STYLES FAN BOOK

**I think you have to take me for me. I am who I am."**

*—Harry Styles*

Harry said he used to pole dance in the schoolyard when he was younger.

• • •

When Harry first signed up for Instagram, the handle @HarryStyles was taken, so he created a profile with @GiveMeMyNamePlease and the owner was kind enough to give it to him.

• • •

Harry had the most solo parts on One Direction's debut album.

Harry once shaved his own initials into Zayn's leg!

• • •

Harry used to be so nervous about performing that he'd be sick before going on stage.

• • •

Some of Harry's nicknames are Hazza, Haz, Curly, and Harold.

• • •

Harry's father is Jewish and his mother is Roman Catholic.

THE ULTIMATE HARRY STYLES FAN BOOK

# Be a lover. Give love. Choose love. Love everyone, always."

*—Harry Styles*

Harry is very ticklish!

• • •

Harry's favourite album is *Astral Weeks* by Van Morrison.

• • •

Harry's album *Harry's House*, is the fastest selling album of 2022 so far (September, 2022). The album's first single, *As It Was* was his second number one single in both the UK and USA simultaneously.

• • •

In July 2020, Harry Styles narrated a bedtime story for the *Calm* app, called *Dream with me*.

Harry wrote most of his album *'Harry Styles'* in Jamaica.

• • •

Harry once spent a day handing out pizzas to homeless people in Los Angeles.

• • •

Harry's former boss at the bakery he worked at said that Harry was the most polite member of staff he had ever had!

In his first school play, Harry played a mouse called Barney.

• • •

Harry and Ed Sheeran have matching tattoos.

• • •

Although Harry is known for his love of parties, he spent his 25th birthday reading in a coffeeshop in Japan!

• • •

Harry used to record song covers on his granddad's karaoke machine.

The last song Harry wrote for his *Harry's House* album was *As It Was*. He wrote it at his friend's house in the English countryside and said it was originally much slower.

• • •

Despite both Taylor Swift and Harry having songs called *Daylight*, Harry confirmed the song wasn't written about Taylor!

• • •

Harry is a huge fan of Joni Mitchell's 1971 album *Blue*, in particular the dulcimer (an American string instrument), and so he tracked down Joni's dulcimer maker and she also built him one for him to play on his *Fine Line* album. You can hear it on the song *Canyon Moon*.

Harry originally wrote the song *Boyfriends* for his *Fine Line* album.

• • •

After One Direction went on a hiatus, Harry started going to therapy, which he now recommends to his friends.

• • •

Harry practices meditation regularly; he said it allows him to be more open with himself and his friends.

• • •

After going out for dinner with singer Stevie Nicks, she wanted to go back to Harry's house to listen to his album *Fine Line*, which hadn't been released yet. Her and her friends ended up staying until 6am!

• • •

In 2022, at his concert in London, Harry helped a fan to come out as gay by waving a big rainbow flag across the stage.

• • •

Harry wrote his song *Falling* while wearing only a towel.

• • •

Harry auditioned for the role of Elvis in the movie of the same name, but the director said he didn't get the part because "he's already an icon".

# Harry Styles Quiz: Family & Early Life

From where Harry was born, to his parents names—how much do you know about Harry before he was famous?

1. What are Harry's parents' names?

2. Where was Harry born?

3   What was Harry's first girlfriend's name?

4   When was Harry born?

5   What is Harry's middle name?

6   Where did Harry grow up?

7   What band was Harry in before he became famous on the X-Factor?

**8** Where did Harry work part-time before the X-Factor?

**9** What was the first gig that Harry ever attended?

**10** What was Harry's pet hamster called?

**11** What was the name of Harry's pre-school?

> "I'd like to take care of someone but at the same time, I like girls who are independent."
>
> —*Harry Styles*

12  What was Harry's nickname at school?

13  What was Harry's first pet?

14  What is Harry's sister called?

15  What secondary (high) school did Harry attend?

**16** What was Harry's first word?

**17** What type of animal attacked Harry when he was 10?

**18** What is Harry's full first name?

**19** What colour was Harry's hair when he was born?

20  When did Harry's parents get divorced?

21  What was the first song Harry learned all the words to?

22  How tall is Harry?

23  What colour are Harry's eyes?

# ANSWERS

**How many did you get right?**

1. His mum is called Anne Cox and his dad is Des Styles.
2. Evesham, Worcestershire in England.
3. Emilie. They started dating when he was 12.
4. 1 February, 1994.
5. Edward.
6. Holmes Chapel in Cheshire, England.
7. He was the lead singer of White Eskimo.
8. W Mandeville bakery in Cheshire.
9. Nickleback, in Manchester.
10. Hamster!
11. Happy Days.
12. Hazza.

13. A dog called Max.
14. Gemma.
15. Holmes Chapel Comprehensive School.
16. Cat.
17. A goat! Luckily he survived to tell the tale.
18. Harold.
19. Bright blonde!
20. When he was seven.
21. 'The Girl of My Best Friend' by Elvis Presley.
22. Harry is 6 ft (183 cm) tall.
23. Green.

# Harry Styles Quiz: Music & Career

1. Who are some of Harry's main musical heroes?

2. What did Harry sing during the first round of the X-Factor?

**3** What is the name of the song that Harry wrote for Ariana Grande?

**4** What 2017 movie did Harry act in?

**5** What was the second single released from Harry's second album, *Harry's House*?

**6** Which actress stars opposite Harry in the film *Don't Worry Darling*?

**7** What was Harry's first solo single, and what year was it released?

**8** What three singles did Harry release from his album *Harry Styles*?

**9** How many Grammy awards has Harry been nominated for, and how many has he won?

THE ULTIMATE HARRY STYLES FAN BOOK

"**Eating toast in the shower is the ultimate multitask.**"

—*Harry Styles*

10   What was Harry's first number-one single in the USA?

11   How many BRIT Awards has Harry won?

12   In which city did Harry play the first date of his postponed *Love on Tour* tour?

13   What award did Harry win at the 2020 *American Music Awards*?

**14** When did One Direction announce they were going on hiatus?

**15** When did Harry host *Saturday Night Live* for the first time?

**16** Which famous actor did Harry replace in the film *Don't Worry Darling*?

**17** What was the name of the song that Harry wrote for Ariana Grande's album *My Everything*?

"I think when you're writing songs, it's impossible to not draw on personal experiences, whether it be traveling or girls, or anything."

—*Harry Styles*

**18** Which fashion designer did Harry become the face of in 2018?

• • •

**19** Harry was the first man to appear on the cover of which magazine?

• • •

**20** What is the name of Harry's current tour?

• • •

**21** Which actress plays opposite Harry in the movie *My Policeman*?

**22** What is the name of Harry's gender neutral make up and nail care brand?

• • •

**23** What is the first song on *Harry's House*?

• • •

**24** What was the name of the Halloween party Harry held at Madison Square Gardens?

• • •

**25** What is the last planned date on Harry's Love on Tour tour?

**26** What two costumes did Harry wear to his Halloween party at Madison Square Gardens?

• • •

**27** Which famous country singer did Harry perform with at Coachella in 2022?

• • •

**28** How many dates did Harry play in the USA on his *Love on Tour* tour?

• • •

**29** Who inspired Harry's song Matilda?

# ANSWERS

**How many did you get right?**

1. The Beatles, Elvis and Coldplay.
2. Stevie wonder's 'isn't she lovely'
3. Just a Little Bit Of Your Heart, from her My Everything album.
4. Dunkirk.
5. Late Night Talking.
6. Florence Pugh.
7. Sign of the Times, in 2017.
8. Sign of the Times, Two Ghosts and Kiwi.
9. One win (Best Pop Vocal Performance, Watermelon Sugar) out of three nominations.
10. Watermelon Sugar.

11. Two.
12. Las Vegas, Nevada.
13. Favorite Pop/Rock Album for Fine Line.
14. January 2016.
15. In 2019.
16. Shia LaBouef.
17. Just A Little Bit of Your Heart.
18. Gucci.
19. Vogue.
20. Love on Tour.
21. Emma Corrin.
22. Pleasing.
23. Music for a Sushi Restaurant.
24. Harryween Fancy Dress Party.
25. Auckland, New Zealand on 7 March 2023.
26. Dorothy from Wizard of Oz and a Pierrot clown.
27. Shania Twain.
28. 42.
29. Both Roald Dahl's character Matilda Wormwood and his friend Matilda.

# Harry Styles
## Quiz: Private Life

Harry has featured in many gossip magazines over the years, usually because of his celebrity relationships! His dating history ranges From Taylor Swift to Caroline Flack, but Harry seems very happy with Olivia at the moment!

1. Harry sparked controversy when he started dating Caroline Flack in 2011. What was their age difference?

2   When did Harry have his first kiss?

3   What illness does Harry suffer from?

4   Which member of the Kardashian-Jenner family did Harry date in 2013?

5   Which Victoria's Secret model, which Harry dated, inspired his album *Fine Line*?

**6** What diet has Harry been following since 2017?

**7** In what year did Harry date Taylor Swift?

**8** Which Taylor Swift songs are believed to have been written about Harry?

**9** Where does Harry live?

THE ULTIMATE HARRY STYLES FAN BOOK

# Age is just a number, maturity is a choice."

—*Harry Styles*

10  How much is Harry estimated to be worth in 2022?

11  Who did Harry endorse in the 2020 US presidential election, despite being unable to vote?

12  Who is Harry currently dating (2022)?

13  Who was Harry's first love, when he was 15?

THE ULTIMATE HARRY STYLES FAN BOOK

**14** How much money did Harry raise for charity during his 2017 tour?

**15** Harry and Taylor were photographed going on a date in which park?

**16** How many followers does Harry have on Instagram (2022)?

# ANSWERS

**How many did you get right?**

1. 14 years.
2. When he was 11.
3. Hayfever.
4. Kendall Jenner.
5. Camille Rowe.
6. Pescatarian, meaning he only eats fish (no other meat).

7. 2012-2013.

8. I Knew You Were Trouble, Out of the Woods and Style.

9. In North London.

10. $90 million.

11. Joe Biden.

12. Olivia Wilde.

13. Felicity Skinner.

14. $1.2 million.

15. Central Park, New York.

16. 47 million.

## *Harry Styles*
# THE LYRIC QUIZ

**Can you name which songs these lyrics are from?**

1. "Trying to remember what it feels like to have a heartbeat"

2. "She said, "Love me like you paid me"; You know I'll be gone for so long"

3. "Don't you call him/her what you used to call me"

4   "All the lights couldn't put out the dark"

5   "It's 'cause I love you, babe; In every kind of way"

6   "Do you think it's easy / Being of the jealous kind?"

7   "Wherever I go, you bring me home"

8   "You can throw a party full of everyone you know"

9   "Brooklyn saw me, empty at the news / There's no water inside this swimming pool"

10 "And I can't take it back, I can't unpack the baggage you left"

11 "Love a fool who knows just how to get under your skin"

12 "I walked the streets all day / Running with the thieves"

13 "Ringin' the bell; And nobody's coming to help"

14 "She lives in daydreams with me / She's the first one that I see"

15 "Walk in your rainbow paradise / Strawberry lipstick state of mind"

**16** "Even my phone misses your call."

**17** "I want your belly and that summer feelin'"

**18** "You can't bribe the door on your way to the sky"

**19** "Maybe, we can find a place to feel good"

**20** "She's driving me crazy, but I'm into it"

**21** "If you're feeling down, I just wanna make you happier, baby"

22  "Don't know where you'll land when you fly"

23  "Don't know why, but it feels so right to me; Something in the way you move"

24  "I don't want to fight you;
And I don't want to sleep in the dirt"

25  "Tingle running through my bones, fingers to my toes"

26  "Wondering, headshake; Tired eyes are the death of me"

# ANSWERS

**How many did you get right?**

1. Two Ghosts.
2. Daydreaming.
3. Cherry.
4. Lights Up.
5. Music for a Sushi Restaurant.
6. To Be So Lonely.
7. Sweet Creature.
8. Matilda
9. Ever Since New York.
10. Falling.
11. Boyfriends.
12. Meet Me in the Hallway.
13. As It Was.
14. She.
15. Adore You.
16. The Dining Table.
17. Watermelon Sugar.
18. Sign of the Times.
19. Treat people with kindness.
20. Kiwi.
21. Late Night Talking.
22. Love of My Life.
23. Cinema.
24. Fine Line.
25. Medicine.
26. Sunflower Vol. 6.

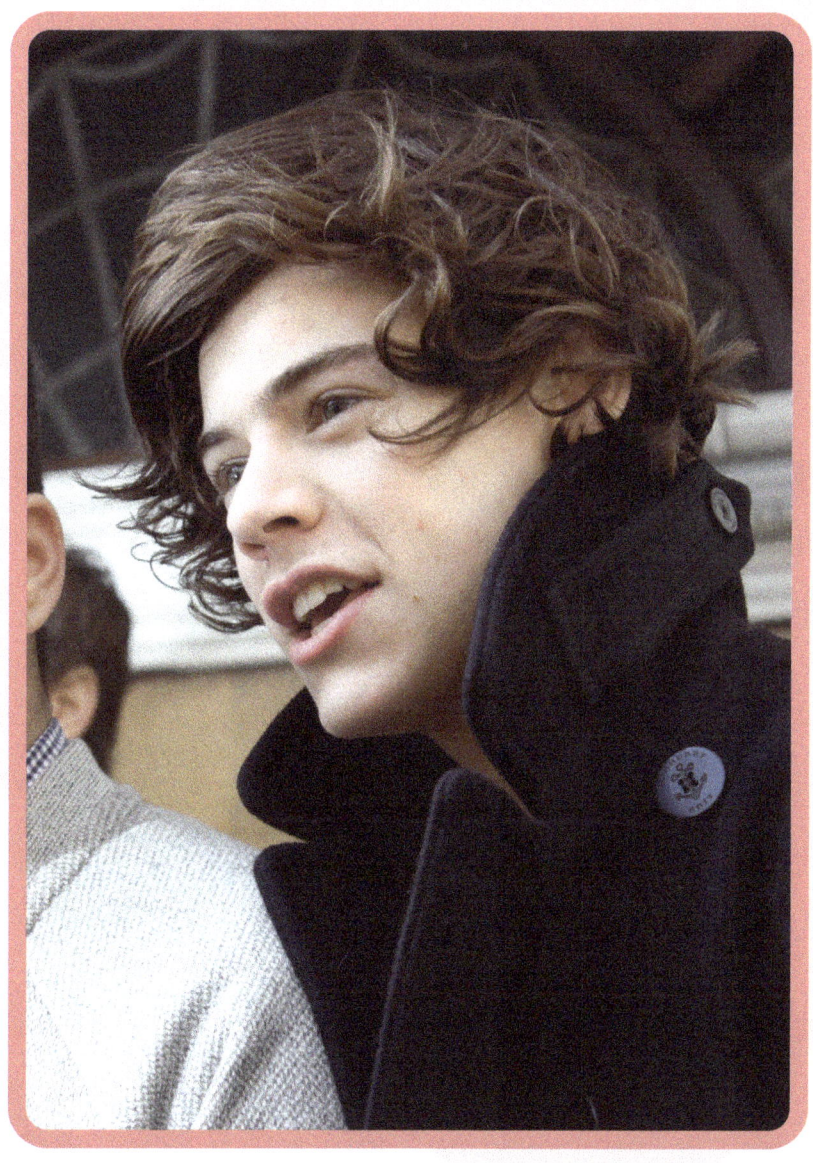

THE ULTIMATE HARRY STYLES FAN BOOK

# Harry Styles Bonus Quiz

Now it's time to test your knowledge on the most random Harry Styles facts. It's going to be tough, so good luck!

1. What is Harry's Twitter handle?

2. What is Harry's favorite song of all time?

3. What did Harry want to be if he wasn't a pop star?

4   What football team does Harry support?

5   What are Harry's favourite colors?

6   Harry has admitted to loving 'chick flicks'. What are his favourites?

7   What shoe size is Harry?

8   What sports does Harry like to play?

9   What is Harry's favorite animal?

**10** What did Harry say he'd choose as his one superpower?

**11** What is Harry's favorite television show?

**12** What is Harry's favorite non-alcoholic drink?

**13** What phobia does Harry suffer from?

**14** What is Harry's motto in life?

**15** What is Harry's star sign?

16  Does Harry wear boxers or briefs?

17  What was Harry's first tattoo?

18  What small instrument can Harry play?

19  Does Harry prefer tea or coffee?

20  Which Disney character did Harry say he'd most like to be?

21  What date was Harry's House released?

22  In which Marvel movie did Harry have a cameo?

# ANSWERS

## How many did you get right?

1. @harry_styles
2. 'FREE FALLING' BY JOHN MAYER
3. A physiotherapist.
4. Manchester United.
5. Orange and blue.
6. Love Actually, Titanic and The Notebook.
7. Size 10 (UK).
8. Tennis, badminton and golf.
9. Turtles.
10. The ability to travel through time.
11. Family Guy.
12. Apple juice.
13. Ophidiophobia—a fear of snakes.
14. 'Work hard, play hard, be kind.'
15. Aquarius.
16. Boxers.
17. A star - he said each point of the star represented a member of one direction.
18. The kazoo.
19. He much prefers tea.
20. Sebastian the crab from *The Little Mermaid*.
21. May 20, 2022.
22. Eternals.

THE ULTIMATE HARRY STYLES FAN BOOK

# *Harry Styles* QUOTES

Harry has always been the funny guy in One Direction—he's always making us giggle! But, he can also be smart and inspiring.

These are some of our favourite Harry Styles quotes—funny and serious!

"A real girl isn't perfect and a perfect girl isn't real."

• • •

"My first real crush was… Louis Tomlinson."

• • •

"It only takes a second for you to call a girl fat and she will starve herself for the rest of her life. Think before you act."

• • •

"A dream is only a dream.. until you decide to make it real."

"I feel like I've woken up with suddenly more facial hair and a deeper voice."

• • •

"I hate the word famous because it has no substance."

• • •

"People often ask me why don't you have a girlfriend. Then I smile and say: I have thousands some just haven't met me yet."

"A lot of the time, the way it's portrayed is that I only see women in a sexual way. But I grew up with just my mum and sister, so I respect women a lot."

• • •

"I'm quite old-fashioned. I like going out to dinner. You have the chance to talk to somebody and get to know them better."

• • •

"I like girls who have two eyes."

"Quite a lot of the girls I get photographed with are just friends and then, according to the papers I have, like, 7,000 girlfriends."

• • •

"Tall girls are hot. Short girls are cute."

• • •

"I've got four nipples. I think I must have been a twin, but the one other went away and left its nipples behind."

THE ULTIMATE HARRY STYLES FAN BOOK

# "I love anything that's a bit of a challenge."

—*Harry Styles*

"I find ambition really attractive too – if someone's good at something they love doing. I want someone who is driven."

• • •

"I think you should not be scared of embarrassing yourself, I think it builds character."

• • •

"I've always wanted to be one of those people who didn't really care much about what people thought about them… but I don't think I am."

# Harry Styles
# WORD SEARCH

| Q | F | A | X | Z | S | H | T | E | E | P | Y |
|---|---|---|---|---|---|---|---|---|---|---|---|
| F | Q | Z | H | S | G | A | Y | U | N | B | F |
| Y | S | T | Y | L | E | S | N | H | G | C | H |
| E | H | F | D | S | A | I | C | F | L | S | G |
| K | J | X | F | A | C | T | O | R | A | E | O |
| Y | U | E | S | M | C | W | X | Z | N | W | L |
| J | H | F | S | D | U | A | E | R | D | Z | D |
| O | H | A | R | R | Y | S | H | O | U | S | E |
| F | Q | W | D | S | Z | K | I | V | C | K | N |
| B | N | T | D | R | E | S | I | C | V | H | D |
| P | T | H | R | C | S | W | H | W | F | T | D |
| O | N | E | D | I | R | E | C | T | I | O | N |

Can you find all the words below in the wordsearch puzzle on the left?

STYLES     ONE DIRECTION     GOLDEN

AS IT WAS     HARRYS HOUSE     X FACTOR

MUSIC     ENGLAND     KIWI

# *Harry Styles* CROSSWORD PUZZLE

Answer the clues and fill in the puzzle —good luck!

**Across**
1. Third solo single.
3. Marvel movie cameo.
4. Birthplace.
9. Type of shop he first worked in.
13. First US number one.
14. First movie he acted in.

**Down**
2. First band.
5. Third album.
6. Starsign.
7. Name of latest tour.
8. Magazine cover in dress.
10. Middle name.
11. Show that made him famous.
12. Sister's name.

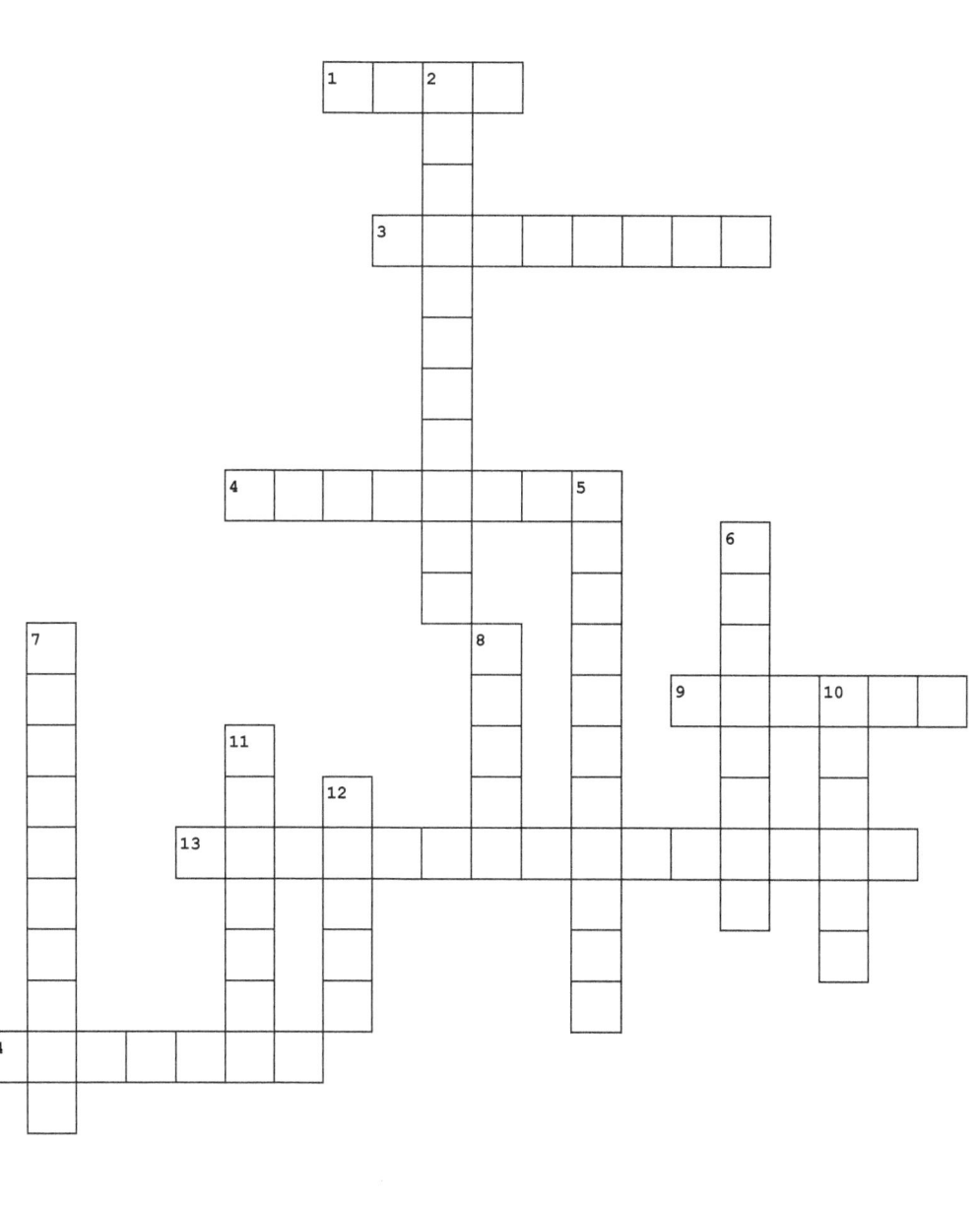

# Solutions

|   |   |   |   |   |   |   | E |   |   |
|---|---|---|---|---|---|---|---|---|---|
|   |   |   |   |   | A |   | N |   |   |
|   | S | T | Y | L | E | S |   | G |   |
|   |   |   |   | I |   |   |   | L |   |
|   |   | X | F | A | C | T | O | R | A |   | G |
|   |   |   | M |   | W |   |   | N |   |   | O |
|   |   |   |   | U | A |   |   | D |   |   | L |
|   | H | A | R | R | Y | S | H | O | U | S | E |
|   |   |   |   |   | K | I |   |   |   |   | N |
|   |   |   |   |   |   | I | C |   |   |   |   |
|   |   |   |   |   |   | W |   |   |   |   |   |
| O | N | E | D | I | R | E | C | T | I | O | N |

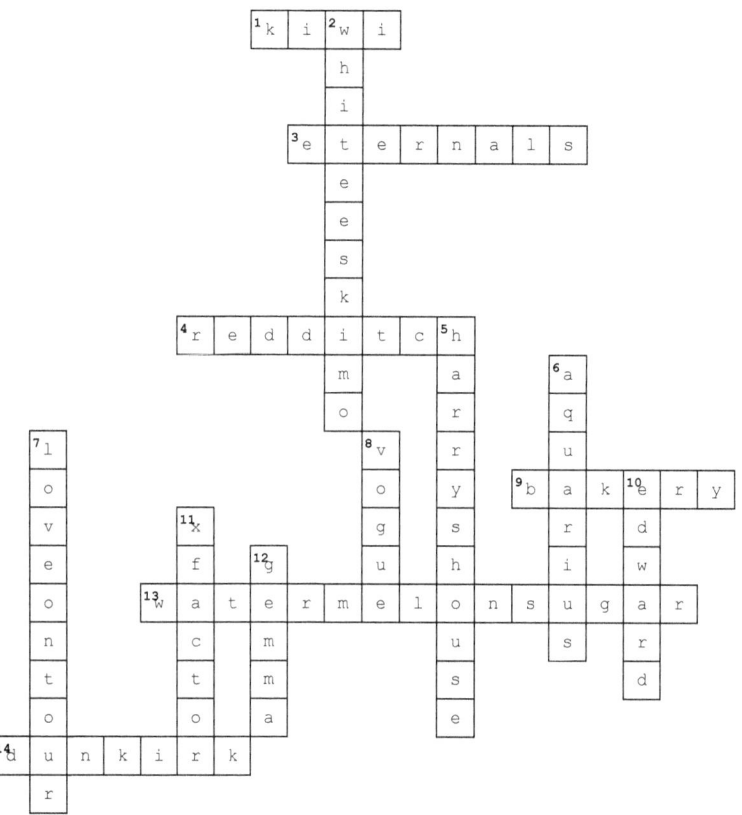

We hope you learnt some awesome facts about Harry! Tell us your favorite in a review—we'd love to hear from you.

Follow us at www.bellanovabooks.com for free book giveaways and new releases.

www.ingramcontent.com/pod-product-compliance
Lightning Source LLC
LaVergne TN
LVHW050135080526
838202LV00061B/6489